RESURRECTING THE BONES

RESURRECTING THE BONES

Born from a Journey through African American
Churches & Cemeteries in the Rural South

Poems

Jacinta V. White

Press 53
Winston-Salem

Press 53, LLC
PO Box 30314
Winston-Salem, NC 27130

First Edition

Cover Art, "Naked Willow Roots," © 2016 by alexsol
Licensed through iStock

Cover design by Christopher Forrest and Kevin Morgan Watson

Author Photo, bio page and back cover, by Kristen M. Bryant

Author photo, last page, Trinidad, by Jenny Scholl

Library of Congress Control Number
2019943439

Printed on acid-free paper
ISBN 978-1-950413-10-2

Your dead shall live; their bodies shall rise. You who dwell in the dust, awake and sing for joy! For your dew is a dew of light, and the earth will give birth to the dead.

—Isaiah 26:19

Many thanks to the editors of the following journals, where versions of these poems first appeared:

Blackberry: A Magazine, "Lands We Travel"

Prime Number Magazine, "Communion Wine"

This Magazine, "Genesis: A Tribute to Rain"

The Transnational: A Bilingual Literary Magazine, "To Damascus"

Special thanks to the Arts Council of Winston-Salem/Forsyth County for helping fund my research with the 2017 Duke Energy Regional Artist Project Grant.

Additional thanks to the Palm Beach Poetry Festival for its Fellowship invitation, as well as 100 West Corsicana and the Navarro Council for the Arts for a grant to participate in their residency. These honors provided opportunities for crafting some of the poems in this collection.

Finally, a heartfelt thanks to my uncle, Rev. Edward LeRoy White, for the long rides down dirt roads, and the stories along the way.

Contents

III.

Foreword

The original title for this manuscript was *Faith of Our Fathers*. After all, the journey through African American churches and cemeteries began with my uncle, one of my Dad's brothers, suggesting we visit churches where my father and their father served as pastors before I was born. With my Dad and Grandfather deceased, I knew this would be a great way to still know them, follow their footsteps, and go back to a time I'd only heard about.

Over breakfast at Mary's Diner on Trade Street in Winston-Salem, Uncle LeRoy and I decided to visit churches on the first Sundays of each month—Communion Sunday. I'd pick him up from his Salisbury home and he'd get comfortable in the passenger seat, telling stories about where we were visiting, interrupting himself with directions for turns. He knew the churches and how to get there by heart (though sometimes getting lost became part of the trip).

Our first stop was a "shotgun" church with a huge tree out front and stones leading to its entrance. The warmth of the church mothers, the ring of tambourines, the hoots and hollers of the pastor and congregation all took me to a different place in my mind. I sat in the pew jotting notes as more of an observer than worshipper, a visitor who couldn't be seen by the few parishioners present. Sitting there in that service, those notes were already turning into what would become the poem "Church Mothers." That's when I knew that poetry would be my way of chronicling and processing this deeply personal journey.

Though this all began with the intention of exploring churches connected to my family, it quickly turned into something larger. The more I shared my vision with others, the longer my list of places to visit grew. The more I researched, the more I discovered the questions I needed to ask, the depths I wanted to reach. In each of the African American churches and cemeteries I visited across twenty-three towns in North and South Carolina, Georgia, and Texas, I felt connected, welcomed, and inspired.

Not every visit to a church or cemetery was planned, however. Once, driving back from Hilton Head, SC, I happened to see a small, somewhat shotgun-style church along a dirt road, and a cemetery to the left of it. I made a U-turn, pulled into the gravel lot, got out, and began looking at the tombstones. It was a Saturday, but the parking lot was full of cars. Moments later, the pastor and another man came out to introduce themselves and inquire why I was there—them in their Sunday-go-to-meeting suits, and I in sweats, holding a camera. Spontaneous moments like this one became critical to my creativity as the journey unfolded.

Other times, church members took me for one of their own. I'd planned a visit to a church cemetery one Saturday in Decatur, GA. I reviewed my research in the Uber from my Atlanta hotel. I walked the land, stopping to study old tombstones, trying to imagine what it may have been like the day any of those persons were laid to rest. I wondered if their families still belonged to that church; if, generations later, those who carried their blood knew where they were buried. My thoughts were interrupted by men asking where to put the table for the fish fry, and what time the program started.

I visited a church not long after the shooting at Emanuel African Methodist Episcopal Church in Charleston, SC, that left nine of its members dead. I wondered, there at the end of a dirt road in Surry County, NC, if the church would feel safe with a stranger popping up unannounced. And even though I am clearly Black like them, I still felt strangely unsteady wanting to interrupt their service with my note- and picture-taking. Trying to be mindful, I carefully approached the pastor as she arrived and told her why I was there. At the end of service, before the benediction, she asked if she could pray for me and my journey, and I welcomed every word.

Not all the poems in this collection were written sitting in a church or cemetery or local coffee shop. Some came before—like "Communion Wine" and "To Damascus"—but it was alongside the poems of this journey that they found a home. They, too, speak to the African American church experience.

Remembering the Black Church as a foundation and bedrock in the social justice and Civil Rights Movement inspired "Ameritudes." Some poems are specific to one church or one cemetery, while others react to the collective experience.

The poems are grouped based on "place," though I'm intentional in omitting many geographical details in order to enable a larger perspective. The first section is built on specific visits to the churches and cemeteries. The second section contains poems inspired by those visits, combined with my experience growing up as a preacher's kid (PK), and the woman I am now. The third section looks at what is happening in our nation, and our world, through the lens of my time spent in African American churches and cemeteries.

This collection is only a beginning. As we think about how to move forward while preserving the past, we must consider a delicate balance. There are unmarked slave and African American cemeteries, others being erased through gentrification, still others forgotten due to ignorance and self-consumption. There is more to explore, more questions to ask, more rocks to uncover and overturn. This book strives to encourage us to both hold our memories with homage to ancestry, and to let go of what no longer serves us in order to make room for the new and necessary. My hope is that what you read will inspire your own journey—internal, or otherwise.

Jacinta V. White
August 2019

Black spirituality has always given African Americans the license and power to express themselves through the sentiments and dynamism of sheer creative and resistant soul force.

—Carlyle Fielding Stewart III

I.

IT BEGINS WITH BREAKFAST

Mary's on Trade

It begins with slow grace. Words pouring over eggs and grits. Soaking up biscuits and Labor Day sun. My uncle saying we should go, like "Thomasine and Bushrod," without the urgency, still the rush to find what we don't know we lost.

It begins with a nod and waving of hands. A midnight train that's gotten off track. A scribbled list of churches our fathers once pastored. We breathe shadows. We mumble hallelujah, moan instead of sing.

It begins with the grief of digging dried blood-soil and buried stories left dead. We drift toward dirt roads overgrown with loneliness, instead; looking for the spot where it first began.

It begins with stories.   Sundays, sitting silently by cast iron pots of boiling water so close the heat makes you itch. The smell of fire cuts deeper than fresh-poured tar. Tears stuck like memories in your bones.

TENDING THE PAST

I am accused of tending to the dead
of tracing empty picture frames

my long-laced fingers before ascending prayers
though call them God I do not—meditatively

weep from longing or misguided grief
I know them no how but somehow

this emptiness is familiar
I make love to loneliness

wake feeling it reverberate between
my flesh and bones

hear it whisper me back to sleep
where the dead call my name

they do not
pray mercy for my soul

or care about this imaginary life I've built
where we eat breakfast in the kitchen nook

I told my mother, as a child, I saw ghosts in the rain
I was sprinkled with holy water, baptized in fire

learned to push secrets under
toil land in silence instead

CHURCH MOTHERS

women in white dresses surround
me after service like absent mothers
longing for baby's return to their breasts

      rejoicing—prayers for a daughter's return are answered—
      while they wait in line to tell me
      they knew my folks, and how they knew me

young, in pigtails and knee-highs, they
remind me when I was not yet full
of the life I now hold

      behind my eyes
      pain taking up space
      I thought no one could see

women, gray curls spiraling from beneath
their cloth hats, twist both my arms in theirs
take her to the altar one says to the other

      I am caught up in their strength
      speechless and well-taught to not
      resist this kind of salvation

we fall to our knees
caught by a purple, velvet cloud
and wooden rails

      blood and water sprinkled on my forehead
      forgive they firmly whisper
      their breath on each of my cheeks

          say you forgive

LANDS WE TRAVEL

We hold lands inside
us like embryos wanting
life. Water. Stones
we have crossed, some
without knowing. Some
forgotten. No matter, they breathe
inside of us like memories seeping
through the sheets, we toss
and turn before our dreams
color. This is us—

Someone's history. Someone's
lifeline. Nothing turns inside of me,
connecting me to its breath, calling
me Mother. Land spans inside
instead, no longer distant,
foreign. Saints have called
and I have responded

like old women—hands up, eyes closed—
Holy Ghost spilled over in Communion
wine cups. I drink
while body broken like lands
open. Somewhere in heaven
my father is praying for rain to fall
on his seeds. Lord, have mercy.
Lord, have mercy.

WHAT WE DON'T KNOW, WE FORGET

Eagle's wing, broken
next to stones, broken.
Sun-rotten headstones
under our feet crumble
into red dirt. Letters faded.

Tell us, who has forgotten
you breathing under earth?
And are you waiting
for the Return of angels
before you rise

to shame us? We have walked by
unaware, taking what you've placed
high for us and shoved it under our unkept
beds, buried. Not saying "in remembrance,"
sacred prayer. Ol' time saints with broken
tongues, religion whole—your names
and rituals faded like morning fog.

We have forgotten—generations
removed—the feel of your dry, broken,
skinned hands upon our cheeks.
Hands to guide us here; hands that built
this on a rock, that laid this cornerstone
sometime between daybreak and dusk.

Your life now between death
and the wake, left as symbols
in stained glass windows and ant-sized dirt
holes for you to breathe. Is it not enough
to pretend there is some connection
between us—now and then—
as if the tie had never broken?
As the bread has been broken, on the same altar
you knelt? As if we ate it together
in the thin moment our lives overlapped? As if
you passed me the cup of wine—your lip
print still moist on the rim?

LEGACY

Imagine them standing at the altar
as they were then—alive, vibrant, holy ghost-filled
thunder voices

Age 11, coming from altar call praying
before mothers and fathers of the church
the *amen*s and *pray son*s

while his own father
looks on nudging him towards the finish line
the only son out of four called that day.

Imagine him, this son, someone's father decades to come
dusty suit and hand-me-down shoes, soles with holes
praying and wondering how

the power in words that come from heads lifted
will change things. Slanting words entering God's ears
takes years to get right.

Imagine this preacher-child's brother, now a man
of his own, taking his niece to stand, to hear prayers absorbed
in the alabaster box. She places her red bottom feet

where her father once stood. Places the box to her ear.
Says a prayer of her own, makes a sacrifice
before moving on.

CHURCH GIRL

After "Girl" by Jamaica Kincaid

Here's what you do
Sit up straight
Place your hands on your knees
Always look straight ahead
Don't turn around to see who is behind you

Stop
Then, go
Get the two quarters and peppermint
From Mother Davis
She'll be waving for you (like every Sunday)
Say excuse me to those you walk by, though they won't move
Say thank you to Mother Davis, loud and clear so she can hear

Go back to your seat
Say excuse me again
And pay attention

Pay attention to the preacher
Pay attention to the prayer
Pay attention to the scripture
Pay attention, girl

Don't pass notes
Don't draw pictures of houses you wish you lived in
And certainly don't laugh
I don't care how funny you think
The soloist sounds

When it's time for prayer and you go to kneel
Make sure the hem of your dress isn't under your shoe
You'll step on it when you get up
And others may find that funny though, trust me, you won't

Keep your eyes open when you pray
But never let anyone know I told you so
I'll tell you why later

And when you open the peppermint candy
From Mother Davis
Don't do it when it's quiet
Do it under a long cough or a tambourine's thunder
When it's time to find the scripture
Don't look around like you don't know where it is
Or that Jesus's words aren't in his blood colored red

When you stand to sing
Sing loud
Let your light shine, girl
And stand up straight

Don't play with your ribbon on your dress
Don't play with your bow
Don't play with the lace on your socks
Leave the buckles on your shoes alone
I looked you over twice and you're fine
Come back this same way

Pay all your offering
Don't chew gum
Sit with your legs crossed
Place your hands on your knees
Remember how I showed you
Otherwise boys will think you're spread like a welcome mat
And their mothers will wonder what I teach you

Put more grease on your arms and legs, girl
I can write my name on your skin like a chalkboard
Look like a lady, girl
Act like a lady, girl
Leave your Shirley Temple curls alone, girl

Remember to keep your hands down
Otherwise people might think you've caught the Holy Ghost
Keep them on your knees
Keep your mouth with a smile
And no one will know
What you think

You never want people to know
What you're thinking
Just keep smiling
Looking ahead
This is what polite
Little girls do

And if someone asks you where I am
And how come I'm not there
Don't tell them
Just keep smiling
Just keep looking straight
Tell them a crooked lie
This is what polite little girls do

HOW TO BUILD A TABERNACLE

Cabarrus County, February 11, 1962

1) You grab the shotgun. You layer the overcoat on top of your nightclothes. You follow the Preacher's Steward and Chair of the Trustee Board who have come to get you. You walk the country block it takes to get there. Though out of breath you do not stop to answer anxious questions onlookers lining the street shout in your direction.

2) After you arrive where you preached just that morning, you walk the charred land. You profess in a whisper to yourself that the church will be resurrected. This is a part of the package—the one you never wanted, but accepted that night when God delivered you from the bed of affliction.

3) Last to leave, you walk home alone. Shotgun tucked under your left arm, Bible under your right. Thinking. Praying. Arguing with God about being yet another example of faith. Your wife and children are waiting at the parsonage door. You tell them it is as bad as you feared. You take off your coat and hat, put up your gun, smell the smoke still on your hands.

4) You document what you've seen: the skeleton of the sanctuary, the crisped pages of songbooks, the scorched cross. Your son asks to take pictures. Your wife takes notes. You call the NAACP.

5) It is night and so you sleep. You dream of dancing barefoot around stones of fire. Through the smoke you see the light.

POUNDS

Sugar, freshly picked greens, corn on the cob, honey, fatback—
pounds of preacher pounding

Prayers answered payments—
pounds of eggs, string beans, tomatoes, fresh dried meat

from the black-owned butcher
    on Depot Street

Poor people rich in gifts walking and carting
their offering of pounds this Sunday

Poor preacher running country circuits two Sundays at a time
preaching good news, praying for ways out of no ways

Signing, "I ain't noways tired"
testifying, "This is how we know God is real"

His childhood stretched across his smile, an uncle
a PK, shares with me across the table

what growing up then was like, points to spots darkened
in the wood where pots sat hot and full

FIRST SUNDAY

He is asked if he wants to come
Take the stairs and mount the pulpit
Sit on its right side

But he has taken off his collar and taken
His seat among the people today
Tambourine playing

Lady, with her grandson, on the second pew
Gets louder, takes up space perhaps others would make
If they had come this first Sunday

I counted more in the cemetery
A stone's throw from the block windows
And hear headstones scream praises

Between the foot taps
On the churchs hardwood planks
(The pianist has called in sick again)

"You are welcome," the minster says to my uncle
And extends his arm to the high-backed, velvet chairs
Above the rest of us

Though he is called by another's name
He is invited because he is reverend
I, who sit next to him, remain

Unwelcomed to enter sacred spaces
Unworthy to come close to the peoples God
I pat my feet as praise to the God I know instead

ALTAR CALL

silent tears | heart revealed | emotions sway | questions denied
quietness prevails | thoughts collide | desires suppressed
words unheard | metaphors spoken | calls answered

love ignored	today's sins
dreams revisited	tomorrow remembers
fantasies heal	souls' amends
sleep pacifies	memories remain
reality lived	forgetfulness blamed
yesterday forgave	kisses felt
knees bent	bodies spent

[   ]

Second African American Graveyard
East Salem Ave & Cemetery St, Winston-Salem, NC

50 tombstones dusty white
a forgotten fog
until we found our way

near the train tracks
I was told, the bridge
to follow

the sounds
the density of our past
drops of red blood dried in green grass

southern dirt buries all alike
dust to dust ashes to ashes
we stand Palm Sunday plain

to get here we walked passed
the all-white church letting out
no one made eye contact

50 tombstones

near the railroad tracks
don't have names
my niece, Erin, is with me

she rubs the concrete
stones with her fingers
we make up names for those missing

and wonder if we are standing on unmarked bodies
if they wish we were barefoot
so they could bless the bottoms of our soles

there is nothing there
just a blank slab to mark the life
of a slave whose blood may live in ours

and on this page

BELMONT, NC

I sit among coffeehouse chatter
a few miles between
generations

& the cemetery

welcomes my inquisition
though "no trespassing"
is bolded

I pretend not to see or hear

the couple sitting next to me talk
Harley's, tattoos, the election
I no longer bother

sip my latte, scribble this poem
the future, this death warrant
reads black and red

tell me what I missed or
let me live where I've already
expired the possibilities

THE ROAD TO SAMARIA, TX

There's one way to get in
but two ways to pronounce the town
we pass from Corsicana to Samaria

When locals ask what I do and why I'm here
I say I'm writing and researching
black churches, the South, burials, unmarkings

I want to walk the forgotten paths of my ancestors
This gets cheers leaving me tongue-tied
I fight through the oohs and aahs

Nod when a couple tells me they want to take me
to see an artist—a black man
who makes illustrations out of scraps

I ride in their back seat, down the partially paved one-lane road
their windows down—her blonde and his gray hair freely blowing
in the wind, my locs twisting like this story, this search, these poems

I wonder if I could find my way back
the road to Samaria is unpaved

RESURRECTING THE BONES

Under baseboards and wooden planks
not yet rotten, there is rocking.

Under the feet of sprinkled church-goers,
church rows are nearly empty.

Generations of pews
leave spaces for memories to bloom

while stained glass windows with family names
in script, shine rainbows

on nodding foreheads. Spirits come
from under foot-patting, get in your bones.

This resurrection comes in color,
quick, twinkling.

I remember hearing
my father tell of seeing such things.

I look to the floor, not above
knowing something familiar, buried

dances through me.
I join ancient hallelujahs.   Empty

myself tomb-like on Resurrection Day
while church-goers stay

seated, sanctified, staring. I know
what's coming, remember the buried

who took my hand, whispered sacred secrets.
This wooden floor is laughing, my toes tapping.

THE JOURNEY

Each visit I take the same notebook, record
observations, names of the deceased, names
of those who I will circle back, next time around,
for a longer visit *over food at my table,* they say.
I date each page, scribble chapter & verse
of morning scriptures, titles of hymns sung,
points of passages the preacher makes
between keyboard chants. I sketch cornerstones
& hats worn by church mothers, take pictures
on my phone of men & children at altars. I keep
sneakers & water in my trunk. Spontaneous cemetery
walks & stops alongside dirt roads calling, *Pull over.*
I remember the time Dad told me he had to pull
over. He heard God speak to him, told him to preach
the Good Word. I remember the morning Dad
pulled over, the time he asked me to follow him.
I remember his gaze upward, the look of God
calling him home. I pull over at No Trespassing signs,
enter places I feel welcome before gunmen rapid fire
between the same walls, pray that the dead are watching
over us if God blinks, only to come to the end, have nothing
to say or write more than this.

II.

12 STONES

I spent Sabbaths
water baptizing
head first
rinsing the week's sin
saying I believe

coming up
dreads drenched
the gospel of Nina Simone
from the bathroom's choir loft playing

while praying generations
will come bathe my back
read my palms
see their history
in the lines around my eyes
smell their trials on my breath

I spent years
walking over graves
bowing to read each stonewashed name
I tucked inside my pocket
12 stones
you ask when I return
if bones can live

listen on

CONFESSION

It's 11:30 a.m. the Wednesday after Christmas or is it
four years ago when I tell you, "I love you," though I cannot
remember your name? You who come to me when I sleep
and tell me not to forget, is it today or a dream
a thousand years ago that I say I won't? "Forget
what you know already. Go to a city that changes everything,"
the sage on the corner of my dream whispers.

"Pinch me." I turn to the stranger next to me on the train
& now it's 4:30 a.m. & I'm walking among tombstones
in Paris, searching for names of black poets who fought
to find themselves here. Or is it 4:30 p.m.? Tell me
about love? Tell me what time it is & I will tell you
what life I'm living & with whom. After

I climbed on the healer's table, I'm asked questions—
"What are you wearing?" "What's his name?" I wonder
why these details matter. I have forgotten, so I make them up,
say what comes first to mind, pretend I am under hypnosis
to conjure you, to feel your spirit move in my bones, to see
any glimpse of you. Before you come again

I will make the bed. I wrote you a letter
on Christmas Eve confessing my disorder.
Have you read it? I tucked it under the pillow
on your side the night you came to kiss me.
The night I felt you sewing up my chest.

LAURA ANN CLEMENT, 1854–1940

Davie County, North Carolina

She made sacrifices as she traveled from plantation to plantation,
from name to name, not sure of her own, from room to room
off narrow hallways in the home that later became hers. She
left petals of flowers now extinct. The slant ray of sun crept
through gaps in the roof.

I'm told the kitchen was her sanctuary; the stove, her altar.
That she mumbled prayers, hummed tunes brought down
from her ancestors. She stirred in a pot on the wood-
burning stove a little herb, a little oil, a little secret.
Congestion, coughing later stirred with fire,
third-degree burns.

She slept with pneumonia since her husband died. No children
around to wrap her in onion-soaked clothes. No one to soothe
her insides with unspoken concoctions. I wonder
if she smelt death coming like the old does rain;
decided it would be easier to lay like the dead.
I'm told the fire turned her charcoal skin darker
than the sun determined just.

Her spirit was left untouched.
I feel it visit by and by.

NARRATIVE. MEDICINE.

I take the stories of you I gather
place them in order

    like rare spices on a shelf

        names from your birth certificate
        the reasons recorded for your death

          dates I hope match
          the dried dirt above

            your body
            in tiny crevices
of my navel
a stone leaves

    the doctors in disarray

        I fill in the blanks
        write my narrative leftover from my great
grandparents

    sweet sweat

    give me

your hands
that had no time to write

and I will read the lines in your palm
see if they say the same as mine

      see whose death will come early
        and whose will soon after be forgotten

      which prescription was written in stone
      and which in blood

GUMBO SOIL

Gumbo soil is great for growing cotton
& blueberries & heirloom roses

but it is better for burying the dead
& stories & roots & family ties

& nonsense & quarrels & letters & coins & cigarette butts
& moonshine & past lives & past wives with boyfriends

& all things unspeakable & guilt & sin & worn shoes
& costume jewelry & faux fur & fake identities & hatchets

& all the harsh language ever spoken to you or against you
words that stink & slay & slash & fly out

all which cannot be unburied, deep
memories & gapped smiles & Southern charm

& lopsided history books & roots of willow trees still
trying to speak, if anyone will listen

& letters in boxes under floorboards & bruised photos
& the feet of your too-late lover

standing graveside tearful & empty-handed

GENESIS: A TRIBUTE TO RAIN

And so this time I listened
Stopped the madness playing
In my mind and listened to its voice
Strong, clear, defined
Jumping from place to place
As though anxiously looking
For a safety net to gather its shattered pieces
Frame it, display it, have people walk by
Study it, marvel it, contemplate, remember it
Pull it up from beneath the dread of day and praise it

The night's rain spoke just the same
As if it was day and so I listened
To it fall without appointment, warning
Direction, expectation, beckoning
It fell in trust, in love
Releasing its fear and feelings
And need to be right
I listened, wondered
What lessons it was to teach me
It called me by name
Each syllable flowing slowly
Like honey over sweet potatoes
I listened unaware that it too
Had been listening
To me   us

It laughed in my face
At what we were defining
As knowledge, truth, God
Still steps behind, ignorant
Of what slow motions our
Minds make deliberating, debating, dissecting
What it means to be here today
You're asking me about freedom

And so I listened
Stopped playing life
Looked up to rain's descent and prayed
For mercy to fall on me
To pass the brick walls and ceiling windows
To fall on me
To pass the guilt and contradictions
The ego and defenses
To fall on me
To pass the confusion and unrealized possibilities
To fall on my tongue
Allow me to taste something pure and holy
Have it pound on my body
Allow me to be re-birthed and enter again
And so today I listened
And it said

Peace be still

COMMUNION WINE

I used to be six, tasting wine from the clear bottle—
small but not small enough for me to hide in both my skinny hands—
that belonged in the latched box sitting on the back seat of Dad's '77
black Sedan deVille wondering how—it tasting like old grape juice—
it healed, how it was going to cleanse the man
Dad prayed about just that morning, before
the congregation and God.

I sat in the back seat of Dad's '77 black Sedan deVille on the
way to the house on the hill that sat next to the House of Prayer,
wishing I drank something that left a better taste
in my mouth, not hot and dry, sticky and bitter like the outside air.
Couldn't help but to wonder how this wine was going to make
the dying man's sins go away, how him having the same
sticky breath as mine was going to bring him
right with the Lord.

I used to be six, sitting in the back seat of Dad's '77 black
Sedan deVille, sneaking a taste of the juice that saved, wondering
how *This is the blood that was shed for you, drink ye*
all of it in remembrance of Me, was going to get this man
into heaven and not hell; wondering how these small drops
from this tube stuck between black velvet like a body
tucked in a casket, meant something so serious
that I would have to wait outside, play with the lace
at the bottom of my dress. And the smell that came
from the dying mans room wasn't that healing but of something
dark and still.

Afterwards, I sat in the back seat of Dad's '77 black Sedan deVille
examining the bottle that once held the power potion, my finger
tracing the rim of the miniature cup still wet from the dying man's
lips hoping to, right then, get what I was told he had received.

I used to be six.

DEATH SMELLS LIKE

old newspapers still folded
scattered over the living room floor

absorbing stories and tears and footprints
of those who wait for the word

wait for answered prayers and to know
if angels exist and what world do the dead prefer

I am ten, maybe nine
when the smell wakes me

though I already knew
it was coming

IN THE BEGINNING

1.

It spoke to her from beneath
and with vivid colors it painted
with flowery words it drew
a picture of a multicolored sun
covered her every step

She walked naked, not ashamed
to her throne   adorned
though for centuries she pretended
to be another her, afraid of being lifted
too close to God

she called it humility
but instead she rejected her true identity
hid the light that otherwise would expose
her darkness   *Let's be comfortable here beneath*
our privilege
she thought herself clever

Then she listened
to it guide her with beaten drums
and chants, and she held her head back
in disbelief at the bold words and sounds
made in her name, in her honor

2.

Today I listened
To you scream for other reasons

Release that which you've kept buried
In your soul since you arrived

Even your moans were unshackled
How did it feel to be torn in that way?

To have the weight ripped
From your ribs and spine?

You screamed for redemption
Time and grace replaced welts with new skin

In silence between our breaths
You asked me if I heard a voice penetrate the stillness

I thought it disgraceful of me
To be seen for who I was

3.

I put it in a box underneath the bed
in the back bedroom of my Grandmother's house

When I visit, I find my way
to sneak a smell, remember the innocence

captured there

I thought it bad to be naturally me
express then, have me repress now
what I wanted to be heard more so than said

I whisper inside
I'll come back to get you
promise
           when deliverance comes

PERHAPS

I bring you into my prayers now
though, perhaps, you've always been there—
in the syllables or tears.
Maybe in the silent pauses
when I didn't know what to say.

Perhaps you were there all along—
in the prayer shawl or knee cushions.
Maybe in the altar rails or mattress
where I knelt; or the fork and knife I held
like prayer beads at dinnertime.

You could have been there
from the beginning
all the way to *Amen*—
in the breath and handholding
the questions that are lived.

Still, I call you by your name.
Pull the sacredness
in that way.

IN THE PRESENT

My dreams were shaped
to the form of your lips
perfected in the light you cast

Shadows of freedom
follow me still
in your absence

My laughter was magnified
and echoed in the tunnels
where you led me

Inside you
I heard and believed
when I covered nothing but my ears

My religion was made
whole and spotless
testimonies real

We were naked and unashamed
I close my eyes and remember
how you worshipped my flesh

The moment before we were born
anew   *on earth as in heaven*
I raise my hands in praise

PRAYER

The sun passes through the cracks in the door,
blindly boomerangs white pictureless walls.
In the corner of dark furniture, I am motionless and invisible.

An ant crawls across the nightstand.
I wonder if it can see me, if it knows
I am watching its small walk, if it is afraid

of me—a shadow overcasting its every move.
There is no escaping the omnipresent.
This is the moment

when I think of you. Is this what you desire,
dear God? Am I to fear you as this ant fears me?
Would this bring me closer to you, like how I am

drawn to a lover's Sunday morning
kiss under sheets, to fear you?
Or is it the obliviousness of seeing you

in the legs of the ant and in the splinters of the wood?
In the notes of jazz that play from my phone as I write this?
Is it the fear of missing you in the silence between

those notes, the beats played to life backwards?
You who wants to touch the soles of my feet with your rays,
are you the part of me that wants to be folded

into the larger parts of my existence, if I just believe
there is more than this? More than what amounts to
the length of the ant's legs if I were to connect them

to this story? To the meaning of life? As some parallel
to how we breathe and move and . . . you know the rest.
Are you the whisperer or the breath being whispered?

On these nights, when the sun is setting, its colors seeping
through the door, saturating lines in wood nurtured before
I was born, like oil, I cannot get deep enough.

In the whispers silence longs to be
within the music that plays
will still come closer?

If not, please let it be because I will find you
are already here, passing through this door
just before the sun.

RE-BIRTH PAINS

I do not remember what it was like to come
from my mother's womb, to be pulled from her
cut belly. I cannot tell you I remember hearing
my own first cry, still covered in her blood,
nor can I say what it felt like to be held close
to her breasts, have her look at me and claim me
as hers, have my father throw his hands
to the sky to praise God. I cannot begin to say
I know what birth was like, but I know
this anguish.

GOD IS WOMAN

I find myself between words—
definitions I do not know
shapes my lips cannot form

I feel an explosion where my stomach
once was   black dust
falling, settling

Here on a tightrope
between beauty & disease
like red leaves falling & butterfly wings

I'm transformed into a guise—
it's complex   the colors of the sunset
before the hailstorm

& it is breathtaking
the way my hair naturally coils
the way God winks at me because Hers does too

I feel a breeze coming
beneath the door I closed

III.

AMERITUDES

Blessed are the ones on boats
who come across seas and under gates

Blessed are the ones who are told they are ungodly
whose language is stripped from their tongues

Blessed are the warriors in black and brown skin
who boomerang slander and shots of fear

Blessed are the lovers wrapped in rainbows
who see no color

Blessed is the past that sweet-talks its way under sheets
of those who dare not daydream

Blessed are the awakened
who stay up sipping tea to see it all

Blessed are the brave
who become gravediggers, truth-bearers and poets

THIS IS NO REVOLUTIONARY ACT

To die is no revolutionary act

blind faith, stubborn seduction into darkness
you follow a voice

and the door closes before you arrive.

While you wait on the other side, someone brings you flowers.
They are not real and no one is there to tell you

if you're dreaming. You feast on worms
or Sugar Daddys

whichever will do.

Silence begets emptiness.

This is nothing new:
   the dying and the burying
   the mourning toil of grief.

But to live is an art
of losing.

THE SLEEPING

There are some who are meant to sleep
and live inside dreams. They come

as visitors to carry
messages from there to now.

You know them. The baby who looks
deeply in your eyes while stealing your heart.

The lover who hypnotizes you,
the old man who speaks in riddles

before falling off to sleep. We shake
them out of selfish yearnings but

do not wake them or chastise them
for not being among the woke.

Some need to sleep so that others
will know what it is like to be alive.

TO DAMASCUS

*Every morning, at the dawn call to prayer, women and
children move silently from the Damascus suburb of Douma
to the surrounding farm fields, seeking safety from the day's
bombardments by the Syrian government. The walk is part
of a surreal routine described by the fraction of Douma's
residents who remain: shopping on half-demolished streets,
scavenging wild greens, carrying out mass burials. But not
even the fields are safe; recently, medics said, bombs killed
two families there—10 people, including seven children.*
—The New York Times, September 15, 2015

I first read this as a poem
my voice shatters
outside myself like it's caught
in a thick breeze of cotton stretched low   a smoke-bombed sky

     I am surrounded
     by glass-bound buildings
     not blown   while greens calmly soak
     in my kitchen sink a few blocks away
           ham hock waiting

Waiting

Each of us silently waits
for a conversion   a call by a name
that alters
sleepwalk and surreal

     I remember

     my Sunday School teacher
     telling the class once
     that we were one
     traveling the same road of life

dandelions waved goodbye
along half-demolished streets
dust on your worn feet
landed at my doorstep
I sweep singing songs
in a language I cannot make out

Moans, like my grandmother's,
coming from beneath my throat
birth those searching   I cannot find
what I lost near this mat   dirty water and religion

I cannot pray
I cannot pray
Tell me, how is my tongue to fold?
How long is it to stay stuck on the roof of my desert-dry mouth?

Shh. How long do we have to be silent?

Tell me, Saul, how did you know
to stop walking? How did you know when to fall?
Tell me, children, what do you see when you dream?
Are you singing, "Lets walk together and not get weary. . . ?"
And will we one day meet on the road outside Damascus?

"Every morning, at the dawn call to prayer. . ."

　　　I first read this as a poem
　　　before collective voices scatter
　　　like cotton-spun bomb clouds　　　*shattering*
　　　inside my palm

BODY

                    sun scarred body coming from between your mother's legs, sixty extra bones scrap her full figured body. in this body you are threatened by your threatening dark skin. i see your dark sky purple grapes massaged by drunkards who refuse to look at your body for what it is. eat the white cracker *drink the purple wine.* "This is the body. . ." they digest hums about being on knees, holding pages of rituals in between shallow breaths. if only it were that easy—shedding sin every hour like shedding 600,000 skin particles. count them. you, reader. can't you see them falling? the bodies? the black bodies? the black bodies of children? the black bodies of husbands? the black bodies of wives? the black bodies of prostitutes? the black bodies of pimps? the black bodies of preachers? the black bodies of poets? the black bodies of the unarmed and unnamed? count the bodies in black body bags and i will count the pages in bodies of works that talk about black body subjugation, about black women body's sexualization, about black men body's derogation.

when i touch your black chest to make sure your heart isn't still, eventually you guide my fingers to read your nipples like braille. i think of the 100,000 miles of blood we traveled into these bodies and i want to know what your body feels like. if it feels like my body. if it feels like you're running out of air. if you feel awkward walking into a room with your body because it's so much like your grandmother's body and your grandmother's body wasn't wanted even by her newborns. or if your body feels like a bullet target though my body doesn't feel like that. i pull your body close to mine every moment i can as if mine is a bulletproof body shield giving warmth so you won't die in my arms or out there later, have your body placed in a black body bag and i get called to identify your body. write your name on a tag with a black permanent marker before they give me what you wore against your body against your black body against your body. this is the body, this is the body, this is the body that was broken.

NOW

I am not in the grave taking dictation
from ancestors who call me
from sleep to bring them flowers,
ends to secrets, or cigarettes

I am not staring at the sun streaming
through stained glass names of someone's
grandparents long gone
past country fields and dirt roads
I've traveled to come to an end

I am not listening to tambourines
or testimonies about the Good Lord
I am not dusting off hymnals
or cardboard boxes holding my deceased
Dad's cologne or journals or hand-me-down hopes

I am not busy making gumbo of religion and sacrifices
while friends sit in the other room
talking about the dryness of their hair
I am not thinking of the hours it took
to get the red clay out of mine
or how the rue is not yet dark enough

I am not looking at midnight against
my lover's skin, questioning where this
will all lead, and I am not wondering
if he sees the tunnel of my thoughts as he travels
the lines of my spine

I am sitting at a window overlooking
the gas station that appeared in my dreams
before I arrived, abandoned, except for
those I meet at 3 a.m., from graves
I visited mid-summer

I bring them cigarettes and ends to secrets,
they give me pieces of myself
they took as ransom before I was born
I wake remembering why I am here
that beneath the bed where I stay is dirt

BENEDICTION

Uncloudy ▮

By ▮▮▮▮▮ the mornin' ▮▮▮

I don't feel noways ▮▮▮

When I look back ▮▮▮▮▮▮▮▮▮▮▮▮

▮▮▮▮ morning, clothed ▮▮ in my right mind, started ▮▮▮

Now ▮▮▮▮▮▮▮▮▮▮ from falling

Rest ▮▮▮ feet

Kneel

▮▮▮▮▮▮▮ burn

Pray for me and I'll ▮▮▮▮▮

▮▮▮▮ honor ▮ my Lord ▮▮▮▮▮▮▮

▮▮▮▮▮▮▮

▮▮▮▮ my story

If all ▮▮▮▮▮▮ are clear

▮▮▮▮ good ▮▮

Let Him have ▮▮▮

▮▮▮▮▮▮▮▮ the valley of the shadow ▮▮▮

I will fear ▮▮▮▮▮▮▮▮▮▮▮▮

▮▮▮▮▮ no music

▮▮▮▮ between me and thee when we are absent ▮▮▮

▮▮▮ Amen.

Notes

Uncle LeRoy and I took selfies in front of each church we visited. He didn't seem to mind, most of the time. Here we are at one of the churches in Belmont. I wrote "Belmont, NC" (page 17) after I visited the area for a second time on my own.

"Church & Field," pg. i. This church in Rural Hall, NC, was one of the first churches of the journey, and where my father served as pastor early in his ministry. At that time, it was a circuit church, one of three Dad served in rotation.

"African American Cemetery, Samaria, TX," pg. 1. Several plots here were adorned with things like an abundance of flowers, mugs and pottery, or a dollhouse. It made me think that whoever left the items felt the buried was still alive.

"Deaconess," pg. 21. This was taken at a church in Mt. Airy, NC. I love how Deaconesses take their time to fold the cloth used for Communion. The act in itself is a ritual reminiscent of burial and resurrection.

"Stained Communion Rail," pg. 41. I found this communion rail in Winnsboro, SC, particularly compelling because of the evidence of its use. Visiting churches on Communion Sundays allowed insight into the individual histories of the collective ritual.

"Cemetery in Trinidad," pg. 59. On a girls' trip to Trinidad—visiting the home of a close friend—I asked to go to a cemetery. My friend's father drove a few of us to the Ortoire Village Cemetery in Mayaro. Even that far away from home, I felt the same sense of sacredness that had become so familiar in the churches and cemeteries of the South. I'm grateful a friend captured this candid photo, as, to me, it represents the journey I hope to continue.

Jacinta V. White is a NC Teaching Artist, poet, and certified corporate trainer and facilitator. In 2001, she founded The Word Project where she works with individuals and groups using art as a catalyst for healing. In 2015, she founded *Snapdragon: A Journal of Art & Healing* to provide a platform for those to tell their story through poetry, creative nonfiction, and photography.

Jacinta's chapbook, *broken ritual*, was released by Finishing Line Press in 2012. She is widely published and the recipient of several awards, including the first Press 53 Open Award in Poetry and the Duke Energy Regional Artist Grant from the Arts Council of Winston-Salem/Forsyth County.

To read Jacinta's blog of her journey as it was taking place, and to stay abreast of what's next, visit www.resurrectingthebones.com.

CPSIA information can be obtained
at www.ICGtesting.com
Printed in the USA
BVHW030309161019
561217BV00003B/11/P